# At the seaside

## Tim Wood

Photographs by Maggie Murray
Illustrations by Sheila Jackson

A & C Black · London

# Acknowledgements

The author and publisher would like to thank: The staff and
residents of Badgworth Court (Mrs Tuck, Mrs Street, Mary
Sherman–James, Hilda Penning, Harry Redman, Mr Pym);
Sharon Poole and the staff of Woodspring Museum Service,
Weston-super-Mare; Sylvia Draycott; the Staff and Trustees of
the Geffrye Museum, especially Vicky Woollard; Paquita
Webb and the staff and owners of Wookey Hole Caves and
Mill; Mr J. Edwards of Luigi's Rockshop, Weston-super-Mare;
Cliff Mills, Laura Spells, Jamil Hassan, Erin Knott, Laura
Hopkin, Paul Watson, Charlotte Roberts, Sheena Roberts, Amy
Hemmings, John Dourneen, Helen Steele and Maureen Steele.

Photographs by Maggie Murray except for: p 13 (top), 19 (top)
Barnaby's Picture Library; p 5 (top) Greg Evans Photo Library;
p 18, 21, 28 Mary Evans Picture Library; p 4 (left) Chris
Fairclough Colour Library; p 24 (bottom) Format (Sheila Gray);
p 4 (bottom), 8, 9 (top), 10 (top), 12 (left), 14 (top), 15 (bottom),
16 (bottom), 17 (top), 20 (top) The Hulton Picture Company; p 1,
24 (top), 29 (bottom) The Illustrated London News Picture
Library; p 27 (middle and bottom) The Mansell Collection;
cover (inset) from the collection of Sheila Jackson.

Published by A & C Black (Publishers) Limited
35 Bedford Row
London WC1R 4JH
© 1992 A & C Black (Publishers) Limited

ISBN 0–7136–3637–8

A CIP catalogue record for this book is available from the
British Library.

Filmset by August Filmsetting, Haydock, St Helens

Printed in Italy by L.E.G.O.

# Contents

# Where do you go for your holiday?

How do you spend your summer holidays? Do you fly abroad with your family for two or three weeks on a package holiday? Perhaps you travel with your family by car, on a ferry across the Channel, then drive to a hotel, villa or campsite somewhere in Europe?

At the turn of the century, there were no passenger planes, package holidays or car ferries. Only the very rich went abroad for their holidays, making the difficult journey by steamship and railway.

▶ St Ives beach in Cornwall. Many people still take their holidays at British seaside resorts.

▲ Holidaymakers returning from a package holiday abroad.

In 1900, most holidaymakers went to British seaside resorts. But only the well-off could afford to go for more than a few days. Most people received no holiday pay except at Christmas and Easter, and Whitsun, the first Bank Holiday which began in 1871. In some industries, people could lose their jobs if they took time off work for a holiday.

4

Very poor families earned only just enough money to survive from day to day. For them, taking time off work meant earning no wages so they could not afford holidays at all. Even better-off workers found it a struggle to save enough money for a short holiday. Some sold their rubbish to rag and bottle shops, to earn extra pennies. Others sent their children out to work at part-time jobs. Many adults worked overtime and paid money into a holiday club which organised trips to the seaside.

◄ Holidaymakers at Southsea in about 1895.

# Time-line

| | Great great grandparents were born | | | Great grandparents were born | | |
|---|---|---|---|---|---|---|
| | pre-1880s | 1880s | 1890s | 1900s | 1910s | 1920s |
| **Important events** | 1876 Alexander Graham Bell invents telephone | 1888 Dunlop invents pneumatic tyre | 1890 Moving pictures start<br><br>1896 First modern Olympic Games | 1901 Queen Victoria dies. Edward VII becomes King<br><br>1903 Wright brothers fly first plane | 1910 George V becomes King<br><br>1914–18 World War I | 1926 General Strike in Britain |
| **Seaside holiday dates** | 1841 The London to Brighton railway line becomes the first to connect a major city with a seaside resort<br><br>1845 Thomas Cook sets up the first travel agency<br><br>1850s Railway excursions to the seaside become popular<br><br>1861 Thomas Cook arranges the first 'package' tour to Paris<br><br>1866 The West Pier opens at Brighton<br>1871 The first Bank Holiday, at Whitsun | Deckchairs, first introduced on liners, reach the seaside<br>● 'Shrimping', using nets to catch shrimps along the seashore, becomes a seaside craze<br><br>1883 The electric railway opens on the sea front at Brighton. It is the first of its kind in the world | 1891 The first traveller's cheque<br><br>1894 The first recorded picture postcard | Slot machines begin to appear<br><br>1900 The 'Box Brownie' camera invented. Photography becomes cheap and easy<br><br>1901 Bexhill-on-Sea becomes the first British resort to allow mixed bathing<br><br>1903 Over 613,000,000 postcards sent in this year | Bathing machines begin to disappear.<br>● Wooden beach huts begin to appear<br>● Ice-cream wafers and cones go on sale<br>1911 Over 850 children die in London in one week during a heatwave<br><br>1912 The luxury liner, SS Titanic, sinks<br><br>1919 The first August Bank Holiday since the end of World War I. The rush to the sea creates chaos, with resorts quickly becoming overcrowded | Donald McGill's saucy postcards become very popular<br>● Bathing costumes without skirts, and rubber bathing caps become fashionable<br>● Big, coloured beach balls appear<br>1921 Choc ices first sold in America<br><br>1922 Thomas Wall begins manufacturing the first factory-made ice-cream |

This time-line shows some of the important events since your great great grandparents were children, and some of the events and inventions which have changed seaside holidays.

| ...andparents were born | Parents were born | | | You were born | | |
|---|---|---|---|---|---|---|
| ...930s | 1940s | 1950s | 1960s | 1970s | 1980s | 1990s |
| ...Edward abdicates. ...rge VI ...omes King. ...irst ...vision ...adcasts  ...World ...II starts | **1941** Penicillin successfully tested  **1945** World War II ends  **1947** First supersonic plane | **1952** Elizabeth II becomes Queen  E II R | **1961** Yuri Gargarin first man in space  **1969** Neil Armstrong first man on the moon | **1973** Britain enters the Common Market | **1981** First successful space shuttle flight | |

...burn
...ons and
...ams begin
...ppear
...untanning
...omes
...ular

...2 The first
...ish air
...rter holiday

...6 The
...ry liner,
*Queen*
...ry, sails on
...maiden
...age
...he first
...ss-Channel
...n ferry
...illy Butlin
...ns his first
...xury
...iday Camp'
...kegness

...8 About 13
...ion
...kers
...tled to
...day pay
...his year

With the outbreak of World War 2 in **1939** many British beaches are closed, and defended against invading forces by barbed wire

and minefields
**1941** Nylon, the material from which many swimming costumes are made, invented
**1946** The bikini invented by French designer Louis Reard
**1949** The first TV weather forecast

Battery-powered transistor radios and the growing popularity of rock and roll music make beaches even noisier than they were before
● Two million Britains take a holiday abroad
● Package holidays become popular. Benidorm in Spain is one of the first important resorts

Bikinis become popular
Surfing becomes a craze in the USA. The Beach Boys have many hits on this theme, such as 'Surfin' USA'
● More families own cars which leads to enormous traffic jams during holiday times
● Gangs of teenage 'Mods' and 'Rockers' invade resorts on the south coast and fight pitched battles

The 'Ghetto blaster' and the 'Walkman' arrive on the beach
● 'Topless' sunbathing becomes popular

**1973** A terrible fire at the Summerlands holiday complex on the Isle of Man kills 30 holidaymakers and injures hundreds more

**1976** The hottest summer of the century so far
**1979** Brighton becomes the first British seaside resort to have a nude bathing beach

Scientists warn that sunbathing is dangerous because of harmful ultra-violet radiation reaching Earth through holes in the ozone layer
● Some beaches in Britain closed because of pollution
● Over 90% of manual workers have more than three weeks' holiday
● Nine million Britains take holidays abroad
● People begin to take more adventurous long-haul holidays to places such as Florida and the Seychelles

**1991** The Gulf War and fears of terrorist attacks on aircraft stop many people taking their usual package holiday abroad, making this the worst year for travel agents since 1945

# The coming of the railway

Your great grandparents probably travelled to the seaside by train. After the success of the first passenger railways in the 1830s, railway companies began to build lines to seaside resorts. The London to Brighton line was opened in 1841. Other 'seaside lines' soon followed.

The railway brought a huge increase in the number of holidaymakers. Seaside towns such as Southend and Blackpool began to grow rapidly. Other resorts such as Sidmouth and Bournemouth, which had no railway, did not grow so fast and became unfashionable.

After the 1880s wages improved and some workers were given paid holidays. Huge numbers of people began to visit the seaside. At first they made day trips on Bank Holidays. Factory workers in the north and Midlands went on day trips to Skegness, Scarborough and Blackpool. Londoners visited Clacton, Margate and Southend.

▼ A group of holidaymakers waiting at Waterloo Station in 1913. Railway companies made large profits from holidaymakers, and many invested in seaside resorts by providing money to build piers and widen promenades.

▲ Holidaymakers arriving at Scarborough Station in 1913. Many would ask the porters or station staff for the addresses of boarding houses or cheap hotels.

Hilda Penning, who was born in 1907, remembers:

'I left school at 12 and went to work in a cotton mill. My sister and I saved up our wages and went to Blackpool for a day trip once a month in the warm weather. It was only half an hour on the train.'

These day-trippers were quite different from the serious middle- and upper-class holidaymakers who had visited resorts before. The day-trippers were boisterous and wanted fun. As a result, seaside towns gained reputations for being either 'common' resorts, noisy places offering plenty of excitement and entertainment for the masses, or 'select' resorts which were quiet places with more sober folk staying in expensive hotels.

Many first trips to the seaside were treats for children who attended church Sunday Schools. Mr Pym, aged 98, remembers:

'I only went to the seaside on day trips. I went with the Sunday School as a prize for going every week.'

▲ The Great Exhibition of 1851 was held in a glass building called the Crystal Palace, in Hyde Park, London. This exhibition of industrial products made cheap day excursions by railway popular for the first time.

▲ Do you think many people would have gone on this trip to Weston-super-Mare offered by the Great Western Railway in December, 1909?

# Somewhere to stay

Where people stayed in a seaside resort at the turn of the century depended on how rich they were. By 1900, most seaside resorts had several large and expensive hotels for the very rich, with luxurious bedrooms, ballrooms, 'Turkish' steam baths and lifts which were originally called 'ascending omnibuses'. You can still see some of these splendid buildings in resorts such as Eastbourne.

Middle-class families often rented private houses. The parents sent their children there for the summer, in the care of nannies or governesses.

In 'common' resorts, the most popular type of accommodation for poorer people was the boarding house. These were cheap hotels which offered only basic accommodation. Families often slept three or four to a bed and shared a single bathroom.

CORFIELD
Boarding Establishment,
WESTON-SUPER-MARE.

South Aspect.

Facing the Sea.

Newly Decorated and Furnished throughout.
Every Home Comfort. Sanitation Perfect.
TERMS MODERATE.
E. & E. WEST.
Bath Room. Smoking Room. Full Tariff upon application.

▲ Postcards from the turn of the century making fun of boarding houses and landladies.

▶ An advertisement for a boarding house in Weston-super-Mare in about 1900.

The Metropole Hotel, Brighton, in about 1893.

Boarding-house landladies provided basic food, such as milk and potatoes, but visitors bought everything else, gave it to the landlady to cook, and ate in their own rooms.

Boarding-house landladies soon gained a fearsome reputation for strictness and meanness. There are stories of landladies charging for hot water to make tea, for example, or watering down the milk to make it go further. Boarding houses were not always clean, either. Guests frequently complained about bed bugs and fleas.

Rules probably had to be strict to keep the boisterous guests under control. Holidaymakers often behaved badly, staying up late, singing and making lots of noise. But many landladies must have been well-liked by their guests, because families returned to the same boarding houses year after year.

Hilda Penning, who is 84, remembers:

'Sometimes we went to Blackpool for our holidays. The landlady was very nice and cooked lovely fish, but she used to charge us extra if we were late for meals. There were lots of bedrooms in the boarding house, but they were very small, like cubby holes.'

◀ A bill for a seaside apartment rented in 1900. Notice the extra charge of two shillings for the cooking fire.

# Going for a dip

Do you swim for pleasure, or to keep fit? Two hundred years ago doctors advised people to swim and even to drink sea water to keep them healthy. In great grandma's day, people had only just begun to swim for fun, too.

At the turn of the century, most seaside resorts had rules which stopped males and females bathing together. Men and women had to use separate parts of the beach and could not go near the areas used by the opposite sex.

There were also strict rules about what people wore. A girl over the age of ten had to be covered from neck to knee and, on some beaches, had to wear a skirt over her swimming costume. Swimming costumes were usually made of serge or flannel, both of which were very prickly and hot. When the costumes were wet, the material stretched and smelt horrible.

Bathing machines at Hastings in 1900. Attendants pushed the machines down the beach as the tide went out. Swimmers climbed down a ladder straight into the water.

▶ These children looked at some Victorian swimming costumes in the Nottingham Museum of Costume. They were amazed by how heavy and big the costumes were.

▲ Edwardian paddlers on Brighton beach in about 1900. It must have been hard for Victorian and Edwardian women to keep their many layers of petticoats dry when paddling. Notice the bathers and bathing machines in the background.

At the turn of the century, people wore their bathing costumes only for paddling or swimming. They did not sunbathe or walk through the streets in their costumes. Changing on the beach and then getting into the water was quite a problem. Swimmers either changed their clothes under large cloaks, called swimming tents, or undressed inside bathing machines.

Today, most people learn how to swim when they are young. But in great grandma's day many holiday-makers did not know how to swim. Some did not even want to learn.

▲ Edwardian water wings. They are made of canvas which had to be made wet before it could hold air. The tube for blowing up the wings is made of lead.

Harry Redman, who is 81, remembers:

'We never learned to swim at school like children do today. We just took off our shoes and socks and paddled.'

dry land

swimming practice --

▲ Learning to swim using a stool.

13

# On the beach

▲ A group of girls playing cricket on the beach in about 1910. Notice what they are using for stumps.

▲ These children examined a deckchair at Woodspring Museum, Weston-super-Mare. In 1900, chairs like this could be hired and taken on to the beach.

At the turn of the century, when people paddled, sat or played on the beach they always covered themselves up. Middle-class children usually wore sun hats to shade their heads. Women often carried parasols or sunshades. Sunbathing was thought to be dangerous and, in any case, pale skins were fashionable.

Your great grandparents enjoyed doing many of the same things on the beach that you do. While their parents or nursemaids sat in deckchairs made of canvas or wicker, reading, knitting or admiring the view, the children played. They built sandcastles using small wheelbarrows and wooden spades. Buckets were not all that common, but top hats were sometimes used to make sandpies.

Hilda Penning, who was born in 1907, remembers:

'We were too poor to have a proper bucket so we used a tin can instead to make our sandcastles.'

Mr Pym, who was born in 1893, remembers that:

'It cost sixpence to buy a bucket and spade. I looked after mine and hung them on a nail in the shed until the next time I went to the seaside.'

There were few beach games apart from croquet and cricket, which was played with a cheap bat, a tennis ball and wooden spades as stumps. Many beaches were just too crowded for games.

▲ Your great grandma might have worn a sunbonnet like the ones these girls tried on at the Nottingham Museum of Costume.

► This girl compared the swimming costumes in a clothing catalogue of 1900 with those in a modern mail order catalogue.

Parents keeping a watchful eye on their children at Scarborough. How many umbrellas can you see?

# Minstrels and pierrots

At the turn of the century, people did not go to the seaside just to swim and breathe the fresh air. They wanted to be entertained as well. On large beaches, there could be as many as 100 entertainment stalls and booths. Punch and Judy was a great favourite with children. Adults preferred the pierrots and minstrels.

Minstrels originally came from America. A band of minstrels was a group of men with blackened faces. The minstrels played various instruments, the banjo being the most popular, and sang songs such as 'Polly Wolly Doodle' or 'Swanee River'. They organised singing and dancing competitions and told jokes.

▲ These children examined a very old Punch puppet.

▼ A Punch and Judy show at Southsea in the 1890s.

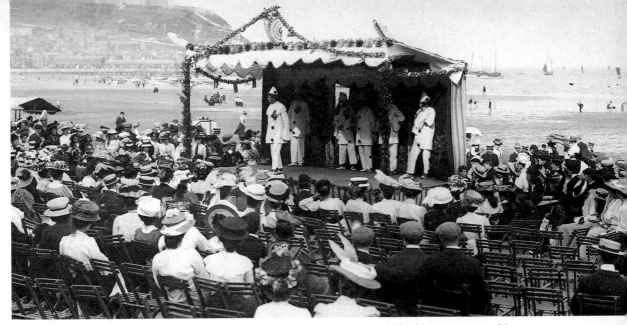

▲ A pierrot show on Scarborough beach in 1907.

Pierrots, who first appeared in Britain in 1891, were musical groups which contained both men and women. Pierrots dressed in costumes decorated with ruffles and pompoms, sang sad songs and told jokes. The entertainers collected money from the audience before the show ended.

▲ Many seaside resorts had bandstands. Bands could play in these even if it was raining. The performances were free.

Every seaside resort rang with the sound of music. Brass bands, with musicians in fancy uniforms, played lively marches. They were often called German bands because the first to come to the seaside were made up of German farm workers. Street musicians played barrel organs, fiddles and bagpipes.

Mr Pym, who is 98 years old, remembers that at the seaside:

'There was always an organ grinder with a monkey. We listened to him playing then put the money in a box on top of the organ.'

▲ An organ grinder and monkey.

17

# The promenade

During Victorian times many seaside resorts were improved and made more elegant. Cliff walks and gardens were laid out and flower beds became a common feature. Floral clocks with the clock face made of flowers were especially popular in flower beds. There were often wide spaces for bandstands or deckchairs.

Unfortunately, the British weather wasn't any more reliable than it is now so many resorts had large 'Winter Gardens' built. Here holidaymakers could shelter from the rain, protected by a glass roof, while they drank tea, ate cakes, and danced to the music of a small orchestra.

The promenade, a long street along the seafront between the beach and the town, was the most important road in any resort. In Victorian times, many promenades were widened and improved with broad pavements and iron railings to stop people falling over the edge on to the beach. Most promenades had benches on which weary walkers could sit and admire the view, and lamp posts so that people could enjoy an evening stroll. Cafés, souvenir shops and special attractions, such as aquariums, lined the road on the town side.

Some seaside resorts built the very latest transport systems, such as electric trams, or hydraulic railways which were driven by water pressure, to carry holidaymakers along the 'prom'. Trippers flocked there when the tide came in. They paraded in their best clothes to see and be seen, and to enjoy the bracing sea breezes.

The promenade at Blackpool in 1905. Notice the electric trams, and the famous tower in the background.

▼ This boy tried on a blazer and boater in the Nottingham Museum of Costume.

These clothes were what every smart young man wanted to wear in 1900.

▲ The seaside was a good place for young men and women to meet. Promenaders often stopped to rest and chat on the benches provided.

# The pier

The paddle steamer, SS *Marguerite*, leaving Margate pier full of trippers.

Many popular seaside towns had piers. The pier was the centrepiece of a large resort. The first piers were often built as landing stages where paddle steamers could stop to pick up trippers for a sail round the bay or a visit to some local places of interest.

The first iron pier was built at Brighton in 1823. During the Victorian period more and more cast-iron piers were built from pre-fabricated parts made in factories then assembled on the beach. During the 1880s, at the height of the pier-building period, seaside resorts competed to build the longest and most spectacular pier. At night the delicate tracery of the ironwork was lit by thousands of coloured lights and flashes from spectacular firework displays.

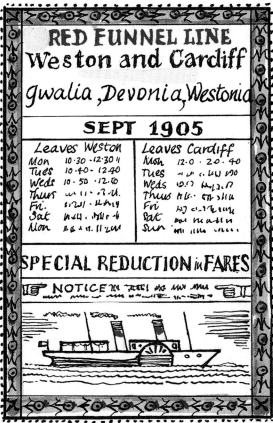

▲ An advertisement of 1905 for the Barry and Bristol Steamship Company, showing sailing times and fares.

20

The private companies which built and owned the piers did so to make money. Holidaymakers were charged a small sum to walk on the pier. A stroll along the pier was like walking on the deck of a ship without the problems of seasickness. Gradually more attractions were added to draw the crowds.

Stalls selling food and souvenirs were built. Entertainers amused the crowd with performing fleas, fortune-telling, trick cycling, juggling and death-defying leaps from the pier into the sea. In pavilions at the ends of many piers, people could have a meal and watch a play or a show or, after 1900, a film.

◀ Strollers on the pier at Clacton-on-Sea in 1907.

▼ Roller skating was very popular at the turn of the century. Skating was allowed along the wooden promenades of many piers. Some piers, such as this one at St Leonards-on-Sea, had a proper roller skating rink. Roller skating was sometimes called 'rinking'.

# Pier attractions

As increasing numbers of holidaymakers flocked to the seaside, pier owners developed new ways of encouraging trippers to part with their hard-earned wages.

By 1900, 'Penny in the Slot' machines had become popular. Blackpool became famous for clockwork models of executions which came to life. Other machines told fortunes or gave electric shocks which, advertisements claimed, could improve people's health. The pictures seen through 'What the Butler Saw' machines seemed to move. They showed what were considered to be rather 'saucy' scenes of ladies undressing.

▲ An Edwardian 'What the Butler Saw' machine like this contains a rotating magazine of photos. As the viewer turns the handle, the photographs flick past and the scene seems to move. Very few people today would find the scenes shown at all naughty or shocking.

◄ A restored slot machine at Wookey Hole Caves and Mill. The children liked the slot machines which showed gruesome execution scenes in which the figures moved.

In the early 1900s, special attractions such as electric railways, switchbacks, water splashes and big dippers were added to many piers.

As the rides and roundabouts became bigger, they were moved off the pier on to a suitable site nearby. In some resorts, such as Blackpool, these attractions developed into enormous fun fairs. Resorts competed with each other to offer bigger and better rides which could attract trippers all year.

Most resorts had model villages, boating lakes, bowling greens, tennis courts, cricket grounds or golf courses to amuse holidaymakers who had tired of the beach, but who did not want to join the hurly-burly of the fun fair on the pier.

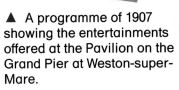

▲ A programme of 1907 showing the entertainments offered at the Pavilion on the Grand Pier at Weston-super-Mare.

◀ A penny placed in the slot of this Edwardian machine at Woodspring Museum made the sailor stagger about, laughing drunkenly.

# Donkey rides and 'penny licks'

There were many quiet forms of amusement at most resorts. Donkey rides were popular with children and adults alike, although women in wide skirts found the animals hard to ride gracefully. In some resorts such as Weston-super-Mare, one of the few seaside towns which still has donkey rides, donkey carts were provided for the very young or the unsuitably dressed.

▲ Donkey rides in 1888. The girls ride side-saddle, resting their feet on wooden platforms. These rides were a great treat to town children who rarely saw any animals.

Harry Redman, who was born in 1910, remembers the donkeys:

'It was twopence for a ride. I lived on a farm so I was used to riding horses. I only rode the donkeys out of curiosity.'

▶ Few modern beaches offer donkey rides because of public health regulations, worries about children being injured, fears of cruelty to animals and lack of interest from children.

Hungry visitors could buy a great variety of seafood from stalls and pedlars. Shrimps were considered a great delicacy and were very expensive. Oysters, mussels, whelks and winkles were cheap and plentiful. They were sold in cones of newspaper or on small dishes and sprinkled with vinegar.

Mr Pym remembers his holidays over 80 years ago:

'Cockles and whelks cost one penny a portion. I didn't like them much, but I did like ice-cream.'

▶ Shrimps and mussels were favourite treats for your great grandparents. The children investigating seaside holidays refused to eat them!

▼ These children went to a sweet shop in Weston-super-Mare. They found they could buy striped rock just like the rock their great grandparents ate.

Other stalls sold sticky buns and walnuts. Lemonade cost threepence a bottle and milk was a penny a glass. 'Penny licks' of ice-cream were sold in paper cones. Vanilla was the only flavour available. Striped rock first appeared in 1850. By 1900, every resort sold pink, peppermint rock with the name of the resort running through each stick.

# Wish you were here

By 1900 a visit to the seaside was, for many people, the most exciting time of their year. Many holidaymakers wanted to share their experiences with relatives and friends by sending them postcards.

Picture postcards became increasingly popular after 1894 when, for the first time, the Post Office allowed privately printed cards to be sent through the post with a half-penny instead of a penny stamp. In 1902 it became legal for messages as well as addresses to be written on the back of a card. This led to a fantastic growth in the number and variety of cards which could be bought.

▲ Collecting postcards is a popular hobby today. Rare cards can cost many hundreds of pounds, but junk shops often sell cards costing just a few pence.

The first British seaside postcards were mainly photographs and drawings in black and white. They showed scenes such as the pier or promenade. They were useful as advertisements for the resorts. Now they provide an important record of what the resorts looked like in the past.

Some postcards were decorated with patterns of sea shells or flowers. A very few were tinted by hand. Gradually, comic and 'saucy' cards, showing fat ladies, weedy men and crowded lodging houses, became popular. Those painted by Donald McGill were the favourites.

Coloured postcards from the turn of the century.

Hilda Penning who used to send postcards from Blackpool over 70 years ago, remembers:

'I liked the funny cards best. The ones with fat ladies on them.'

▶ This postcard of the *Walton Belle* steamer was actually an advertisement for the Belle Steamer Company.

**BELLE STEAMERS.**

THIS SPACE AS WELL AS THE BACK MAY
Daily Sailings (Fridays excepted)
to Southend, Clacton, Walton,
Felixstowe, Southwold, Lowestoft,
Gorleston, Yarmouth, Margate,
Ramsgate, &c., &c.,

**CHEAP TRIPS**

| | | |
|---|---|---|
| Day Return. Saloon. | TO | Season Return. F. Cabin Saloon. |
| | SOUTHEND | 3/- & 3/6 |
| 4/6 | CLACTON or | 5/- ,, 6/- |
| | WALTON | 5/6 ,, 6/6 |
| 5/- | MARGATE | 5/- ,, 6/- |
| — | RAMSGATE | 5/6 ,, 6/6 |

Time Tables and "Where to Stay," post free from :—
"BELLE HOUSE,"
Fish Street Hill, E.C.

◀ There was nowhere to write a message on the reverse of the card. Instead, the company printed the prices of its fares.

27

# Souvenirs

Do you buy souvenirs when you go on holiday? Your great grandparents certainly did. By 1900 a large industry had sprung up, producing a huge variety of seaside souvenirs. The most popular souvenirs were cheap to buy and bright enough to bring back the memory of a summer holiday during the winter months.

Pottery and china were very popular. One very successful British manufacturer was William Goss, who produced souvenir items decorated with the coats of arms of seaside resorts. But most souvenir china was made in Germany. Pieces were often decorated with pictures of the resort and a suitable motto, such as 'A present from Skegness'.

▼ A 'trippers' store' or souvenir shop at Morecambe in about 1910.

▲ Some china souvenirs, similar to those which were popular at the turn of the century.

One form of souvenir which increased in popularity after 1900 was the photograph. The first cheap camera, the 'Box Brownie', was made in 1900 and started a craze for 'holiday snaps'.

▲ A Victorian picture made from seaweed and shells.

Other souvenirs were made from wood, shells, glass and seaweed. Collecting shells was a popular pastime. Visitors collected them to decorate picture frames and mirrors. Local people spent the winter decorating boxes and plates with shells to sell as souvenirs in the summer. Seaweed was used to make pictures. In places such as Lyme Regis, fossil hunting became popular and fossils were collected or bought as souvenirs.

▲ This girl tried out a 'Box Brownie' camera in the Woodspring Museum, Weston-super-Mare. She found it very hard to see through the tiny viewfinder.

◄ A beach photographer at work in 1892. He needs two assistants – one to hold up a light reflector and the other to blow a toy trumpet to distract the child while he takes the photo.

# How to find out more

| Start here | To find out about... | Who will have... |
|---|---|---|
| Old people | Seaside holidays at the turn of the century | Old photos, scrap books, memories, souvenirs |
| Museums | Old things to look at and possibly handle | Reconstructed piers and seaside scenes, displays of objects connected with seaside holidays |
| Libraries | ● Loan collections<br>● Reference collections<br>● Information to help your research<br>● Local history section | ● Books to borrow<br>● Books, magazines, newspapers<br>● Useful addresses, guidebooks, additional reference material<br>● Newspapers and guides to look at; photographs of local holidaymakers; tape recordings of old people remembering their holidays |
| Manufacturers of products connected with seaside holidays | History of their products | Booklets, pictures, advertisements and information about the history of their products |
| Junk shops | What people bought | Old postcards and old magazines showing holiday scenes. Old souvenirs |
| Local history society | Your area a hundred years ago | Information, reference material, and advice on how to further your research |

# Who can tell you more?

They can. Use a tape recorder for recording their memories. Handle anything they show you with great care and if they lend you something, label it with their name and keep it somewhere safe.

The curator or the museum's education officer. Many museums have bookshops and a notice board where you can look for further information

- The librarian
- The reference librarian
- Ask the archivist for the name and address of the local history society

The Public Relations Officer of the company, part of whose job is to help with queries like yours

The owner. Specialist shopkeepers are very enthusiastic and knowledgeable about their stock. They may know of local people with collections of things connected with seaside holidays. They may be able to give you further contacts and addresses

The secretary

# Places to visit

The following places have displays, reconstructions or exhibitions connected with seaside holidays:

*Bognor Regis Local History Museum*, Hotham Park Lodge, High Street, Bognor Regis, West Sussex PO21 1HW.
*Broughty Castle Museum*, Broughty Ferry, Near Dundee, Angus. Tel: 0383 76121.
*Cromer Museum*, East Cottages, Tucker Street, Cromer, Norfolk NR11 7PD. Tel: 0263 513543.
*Llandrindod Wells Museum*, Temple Street, Llandrindod Wells, Powys. Tel: 0597 4513.
*Museum of Local History*, Westham Road, Weymouth, Dorset DT4 8NF. Tel: 0305 774246.
*Old Town Hall Museum of Local History*, High Street, Hastings, East Sussex TN34 3EW. Tel: 0424 425855.
*Ramsgate Museum*, Ramsgate Library, Guildford Lawn, Ramsgate, Kent CT11 9AY. Tel: 0843 593532.
*Royal National Lifeboat Institution*, Zetland Lifeboat Museum, Old Lifeboat House, King Street, Redcar, Cleveland TS10 3AG.
*Southampton Maritime Museum*, The Wool House, Town Quay, Southampton. Tel: 0703 223941.
*Tollhouse Museum*, Tollhouse Street, Great Yarmouth, Norfolk NR30 2SQ. Tel: 0493 858900.
*Woodspring Museum*, Burlington Street, Weston-super-Mare, Avon BS23 1PR. Tel: 0934 21028.
*Wookey Hole Caves and Mill*, Wookey Hole, Wells, Somerset BA5 1BB. Tel: 0749 72243.

Many seaside resorts have small museums containing sections devoted to life there at the turn of the century and will have some material and artefacts related to holidays. Some transport museums may also have displays connected with excursions and trippers.

# Index